If Lost, Please Return To:

_____

YOU ARE

God's

MASTERPIECE

Monday

Today's Goals

Do my bible study
Put up clean clothes
Walk at least 20 min

Tuesday

Today's Goals

Wednesday

Today's Goals

Thursday

Today's Goals

Friday

Today's Goals

_____

_____

_____

_____

Saturday

Today's Goals

_____

_____

_____

_____

_____

Sunday

Today's Goals

_____

_____

_____

_____

Notes

_____

_____

_____

_____

_____

Bible Study

Date: 6-28-21

Today's Study

Scripture

Romans 12:2

~~Therefore I urge you~~
~~brothers,~~ in view of
~~God's~~ mercy,
Do not conform any
longer to the pattern
of this world, but
be transformed by
the RENEWING of
your mind. Then you
will be able to ~~test~~
and approve of God's
will is - his good, pleasing
(what)
and perfect will.

Praise

Prayer

S.O.A.P.

Scripture

Romans 12:2 NLT
Don't copy the behavior and customs of this world, but let God transform you into a new person by changing the way you think. Then you will learn to know God's will for you, which is good, pleasing & perfect.

Observation

We have to transform our minds by not listening to the world, but to God. The devil is always trying to take us down and it all starts with my thoughts.

Application

I have to take every thought captive. Take the (-) and replace with (+) with the word of God.

Prayer

Lord,
Please give me rest, peace, and give me the tools to help conform my mind and let me thoughts be fixed on you.

Reflection

What Is This Scripture Telling Me?

_____

_____

_____

_____

Why Did God Include This Scripture In The Bible?

_____

_____

_____

_____

What Do I Need To Further Study From This Verse?

_____

_____

_____

_____

Bible Study   Date:

Today's Study

Scripture

_____

_____

_____

_____

_____

_____

_____

_____

_____

_____

_____

_____

_____

_____

_____

_____

_____

Praise

Prayer

S.O.A.P.

Scripture

Observation

Application

Prayer

Reflection

What Is This Scripture Telling Me?

_____

_____

_____

_____

Why Did God Include This Scripture In The Bible?

_____

_____

_____

_____

What Do I Need To Further Study From This Verse?

_____

_____

_____

_____

Bible Study

Date:

Today's Study

Scripture

_____

_____

_____

_____

_____

_____

_____

_____

_____

_____

_____

_____

_____

_____

_____

_____

_____

_____

Praise

Prayer

S.O.A.P.

Scripture	Observation

Application	Prayer

Reflection

What Is This Scripture Telling Me?

_____

_____

_____

_____

Why Did God Include This Scripture In The Bible?

_____

_____

_____

_____

What Do I Need To Further Study From This Verse?

_____

_____

_____

_____

Bible Study

Date:

Today's Study

Scripture

Praise

Prayer

S.O.A.P.

Scripture

Observation

Application

Prayer

Reflection

What Is This Scripture Telling Me?

_____

_____

_____

_____

_____

Why Did God Include This Scripture In The Bible?

_____

_____

_____

_____

_____

What Do I Need To Further Study From This Verse?

_____

_____

_____

_____

_____

Bible Study

Date:

Today's Study

Scripture

Praise

Prayer

S.O.A.P.

Scripture

Observation

Application

Prayer

Reflection

What Is This Scripture Telling Me?

_____

_____

_____

_____

Why Did God Include This Scripture In The Bible?

_____

_____

_____

_____

What Do I Need To Further Study From This Verse?

_____

_____

_____

_____

Bible Study

Date:

Today's Study

Scripture

Praise

Prayer

S.O.A.P.

Scripture

Observation

Application

Prayer

Reflection

What Is This Scripture Telling Me?

_____

_____

_____

_____

Why Did God Include This Scripture In The Bible?

_____

_____

_____

_____

What Do I Need To Further Study From This Verse?

_____

_____

_____

_____

Bible Study   Date:

Today's Study

Scripture

_____
_____
_____
_____
_____
_____
_____
_____
_____
_____
_____
_____
_____
_____
_____
_____
_____
_____
_____

Praise

Prayer

S.O.A.P.

Scripture	Observation

Application	Prayer

Reflection

What Is This Scripture Telling Me?

_____

_____

_____

_____

Why Did God Include This Scripture In The Bible?

_____

_____

_____

_____

What Do I Need To Further Study From This Verse?

_____

_____

_____

_____

Monday

Today's Goals

_____
_____
_____
_____

Tuesday

Today's Goals

_____
_____
_____
_____

Wednesday

Today's Goals

_____
_____
_____
_____

Thursday

Today's Goals

_____
_____
_____
_____

Friday

Today's Goals

_____
_____
_____
_____

Saturday

Today's Goals

_____
_____
_____
_____

Sunday

Today's Goals

_____
_____
_____
_____

Notes

_____
_____
_____
_____

Bible Study

Date:

Today's Study

Scripture

Praise

Prayer

S.O.A.P.

Scripture

Observation

Application

Prayer

Reflection

What Is This Scripture Telling Me?

_____

_____

_____

_____

Why Did God Include This Scripture In The Bible?

_____

_____

_____

_____

What Do I Need To Further Study From This Verse?

_____

_____

_____

_____

Bible Study

Date:

Today's Study

Scripture

_____

Praise

Prayer

S.O.A.P.

Scripture

Observation

Application

Prayer

Reflection

What Is This Scripture Telling Me?

_____

_____

_____

_____

Why Did God Include This Scripture In The Bible?

_____

_____

_____

_____

What Do I Need To Further Study From This Verse?

_____

_____

_____

_____

Bible Study

Date:

Today's Study

Scripture

Praise

Prayer

S.O.A.P.

Scripture

Observation

Application

Prayer

Reflection

What Is This Scripture Telling Me?

_____

_____

_____

_____

_____

Why Did God Include This Scripture In The Bible?

_____

_____

_____

_____

_____

What Do I Need To Further Study From This Verse?

_____

_____

_____

_____

_____

Bible Study   Date:

Today's Study

Scripture

_____

_____

_____

_____

_____

_____

_____

_____

_____

_____

_____

_____

_____

_____

_____

_____

_____

_____

Praise

Prayer

S.O.A.P.

Scripture

Observation

Application

Prayer

Reflection

What Is This Scripture Telling Me?

_____

_____

_____

_____

Why Did God Include This Scripture In The Bible?

_____

_____

_____

_____

What Do I Need To Further Study From This Verse?

_____

_____

_____

_____

Bible Study

Date:

Today's Study

Scripture

_____

_____

_____

_____

_____

_____

_____

_____

_____

_____

_____

_____

_____

_____

_____

_____

Praise

Prayer

S.O.A.P.

Scripture

Observation

Application

Prayer

Reflection

What Is This Scripture Telling Me?

_____

_____

_____

_____

Why Did God Include This Scripture In The Bible?

_____

_____

_____

_____

What Do I Need To Further Study From This Verse?

_____

_____

_____

_____

Bible Study

Date:

Today's Study

Scripture

_____

_____

_____

_____

_____

_____

_____

_____

_____

_____

_____

_____

_____

_____

_____

_____

_____

_____

Praise

Prayer

S.O.A.P.

Scripture	Observation

Application	Prayer

Reflection

What Is This Scripture Telling Me?

_____

_____

_____

_____

Why Did God Include This Scripture In The Bible?

_____

_____

_____

_____

What Do I Need To Further Study From This Verse?

_____

_____

_____

_____

Bible Study Date:

Today's Study

Scripture

Praise

Prayer

S.O.A.P.

Scripture

Observation

Application

Prayer

Reflection

What Is This Scripture Telling Me?

_____

_____

_____

_____

Why Did God Include This Scripture In The Bible?

_____

_____

_____

_____

What Do I Need To Further Study From This Verse?

_____

_____

_____

_____

Monday

Today's Goals

_____

_____

_____

_____

Tuesday

Today's Goals

_____

_____

_____

_____

Wednesday

Today's Goals

_____

_____

_____

_____

Thursday

Today's Goals

_____

_____

_____

_____

Friday

Today's Goals

Saturday

Today's Goals

Sunday

Today's Goals

Notes

Bible Study

Date:

Today's Study

Scripture

Praise

Prayer

S.O.A.P.

Scripture	Observation

Application	Prayer

Reflection

What Is This Scripture Telling Me?

_____

_____

_____

_____

Why Did God Include This Scripture In The Bible?

_____

_____

_____

_____

What Do I Need To Further Study From This Verse?

_____

_____

_____

_____

Bible Study

Date:

Today's Study

Scripture

Praise

Prayer

S.O.A.P.

Scripture

Observation

Application

Prayer

Reflection

What Is This Scripture Telling Me?

_____

_____

_____

_____

Why Did God Include This Scripture In The Bible?

_____

_____

_____

_____

What Do I Need To Further Study From This Verse?

_____

_____

_____

_____

Bible Study

Date:

Today's Study

Scripture

Praise

Prayer

S.O.A.P.

Scripture

Observation

Application

Prayer

Reflection

What Is This Scripture Telling Me?

_____

_____

_____

_____

Why Did God Include This Scripture In The Bible?

_____

_____

_____

_____

What Do I Need To Further Study From This Verse?

_____

_____

_____

_____

Bible Study

Date:

Today's Study

Scripture

_____

_____

_____

_____

_____

_____

_____

_____

_____

_____

_____

_____

_____

_____

_____

_____

Praise

Prayer

S.O.A.P.

Scripture

Observation

Application

Prayer

Reflection

What Is This Scripture Telling Me?

_____

_____

_____

_____

Why Did God Include This Scripture In The Bible?

_____

_____

_____

_____

What Do I Need To Further Study From This Verse?

_____

_____

_____

_____

Bible Study

Date:

Today's Study

Scripture

Praise

Prayer

S.O.A.P.

Scripture

Observation

Application

Prayer

Reflection

What Is This Scripture Telling Me?

_____

_____

_____

_____

Why Did God Include This Scripture In The Bible?

_____

_____

_____

_____

What Do I Need To Further Study From This Verse?

_____

_____

_____

_____

Bible Study Date:

Today's Study

Scripture

Praise

Prayer

S.O.A.P.

Scripture

Observation

Application

Prayer

Reflection

What Is This Scripture Telling Me?

_____

_____

_____

_____

Why Did God Include This Scripture In The Bible?

_____

_____

_____

_____

What Do I Need To Further Study From This Verse?

_____

_____

_____

_____

Bible Study

Date:

Today's Study

Scripture

_____

_____

_____

_____

_____

_____

_____

_____

_____

_____

_____

_____

_____

_____

_____

_____

Praise

Prayer

S.O.A.P.

Scripture	Observation

Application	Prayer

Reflection

What Is This Scripture Telling Me?

_____

_____

_____

_____

Why Did God Include This Scripture In The Bible?

_____

_____

_____

_____

What Do I Need To Further Study From This Verse?

_____

_____

_____

_____

Monday

Today's Goals

_____

_____

_____

_____

Tuesday

Today's Goals

_____

_____

_____

_____

Wednesday

Today's Goals

_____

_____

_____

_____

Thursday

Today's Goals

_____

_____

_____

_____

Friday

Today's Goals

Saturday

Today's Goals

Sunday

Today's Goals

Notes

Bible Study Date:

Today's Study

Scripture

Praise

Prayer

S.O.A.P.

Scripture

Observation

Application

Prayer

Reflection

What Is This Scripture Telling Me?

_____

_____

_____

_____

Why Did God Include This Scripture In The Bible?

_____

_____

_____

_____

What Do I Need To Further Study From This Verse?

_____

_____

_____

_____

Bible Study

Date:

Today's Study

Scripture

Praise

Prayer

S.O.A.P.

Scripture

Observation

Application

Prayer

Reflection

What Is This Scripture Telling Me?

_____

_____

_____

_____

Why Did God Include This Scripture In The Bible?

_____

_____

_____

_____

What Do I Need To Further Study From This Verse?

_____

_____

_____

_____

Bible Study

Date:

Today's Study

Scripture

Praise

Prayer

S.O.A.P.

Scripture

Observation

Application

Prayer

Reflection

What Is This Scripture Telling Me?

_____

_____

_____

_____

Why Did God Include This Scripture In The Bible?

_____

_____

_____

_____

What Do I Need To Further Study From This Verse?

_____

_____

_____

_____

Bible Study

Date:

Today's Study

Scripture

Praise

Prayer

S.O.A.P.

Scripture

Observation

Application

Prayer

Reflection

What Is This Scripture Telling Me?

_____

_____

_____

_____

Why Did God Include This Scripture In The Bible?

_____

_____

_____

_____

What Do I Need To Further Study From This Verse?

_____

_____

_____

_____

Bible Study Date:

Today's Study

Scripture

Praise

Prayer

S.O.A.P.

Scripture

Observation

Application

Prayer

Reflection

What Is This Scripture Telling Me?

_____

_____

_____

_____

Why Did God Include This Scripture In The Bible?

_____

_____

_____

_____

What Do I Need To Further Study From This Verse?

_____

_____

_____

_____

Bible Study

Date:

Today's Study

Scripture

Praise

Prayer

S.O.A.P.

Scripture

Observation

Application

Prayer

Reflection

What Is This Scripture Telling Me?

_____

_____

_____

_____

Why Did God Include This Scripture In The Bible?

_____

_____

_____

_____

What Do I Need To Further Study From This Verse?

_____

_____

_____

_____

Bible Study

Date:

Today's Study

Scripture

Praise

Prayer

S.O.A.P.

Scripture

Observation

Application

Prayer

Reflection

What Is This Scripture Telling Me?

_____

_____

_____

_____

Why Did God Include This Scripture In The Bible?

_____

_____

_____

_____

What Do I Need To Further Study From This Verse?

_____

_____

_____

_____

Monday

Today's Goals

_____

_____

_____

_____

Tuesday

Today's Goals

_____

_____

_____

_____

Wednesday

Today's Goals

_____

_____

_____

_____

Thursday

Today's Goals

_____

_____

_____

_____

Friday

Today's Goals

_____

_____

_____

_____

Saturday

Today's Goals

_____

_____

_____

_____

Sunday

Today's Goals

_____

_____

_____

_____

Notes

_____

_____

_____

_____

_____

Bible Study

Date:

Today's Study

Scripture

_____

_____

_____

_____

_____

_____

_____

_____

_____

_____

_____

_____

_____

_____

_____

_____

Praise

Prayer

S.O.A.P.

Scripture

Observation

Application

Prayer

Reflection

What Is This Scripture Telling Me?

_____

_____

_____

_____

Why Did God Include This Scripture In The Bible?

_____

_____

_____

_____

What Do I Need To Further Study From This Verse?

_____

_____

_____

_____

Bible Study
Date:

Today's Study

Scripture

_____
_____
_____
_____
_____
_____
_____
_____
_____

_____
_____
_____
_____
_____
_____
_____
_____

Praise

Prayer

S.O.A.P.

Scripture

Observation

Application

Prayer

Reflection

What Is This Scripture Telling Me?

_____

_____

_____

_____

Why Did God Include This Scripture In The Bible?

_____

_____

_____

_____

What Do I Need To Further Study From This Verse?

_____

_____

_____

_____

Bible Study Date:

Today's Study

Scripture

Praise

Prayer

S.O.A.P.

Scripture

Observation

Application

Prayer

Reflection

What Is This Scripture Telling Me?

_____

_____

_____

_____

Why Did God Include This Scripture In The Bible?

_____

_____

_____

_____

What Do I Need To Further Study From This Verse?

_____

_____

_____

_____

Bible Study

Date:

Today's Study

Scripture

_____

_____

_____

_____

_____

_____

_____

_____

_____

_____

_____

_____

_____

_____

_____

_____

Praise

Prayer

S.O.A.P.

Scripture

Observation

Application

Prayer

Reflection

What Is This Scripture Telling Me?

_____

_____

_____

_____

Why Did God Include This Scripture In The Bible?

_____

_____

_____

_____

What Do I Need To Further Study From This Verse?

_____

_____

_____

_____

Bible Study

Date:

Today's Study

Scripture

Praise

Prayer

S.O.A.P.

Scripture

Observation

Application

Prayer

Reflection

What Is This Scripture Telling Me?

_____

_____

_____

_____

Why Did God Include This Scripture In The Bible?

_____

_____

_____

_____

What Do I Need To Further Study From This Verse?

_____

_____

_____

_____

Bible Study Date:

Today's Study

Scripture

Praise

Prayer

S.O.A.P.

Scripture	Observation

Application	Prayer

Reflection

What Is This Scripture Telling Me?

_____

_____

_____

_____

Why Did God Include This Scripture In The Bible?

_____

_____

_____

_____

What Do I Need To Further Study From This Verse?

_____

_____

_____

_____

Bible Study

Date:

Today's Study

Scripture

Praise

Prayer

S.O.A.P.

Scripture

Observation

Application

Prayer

Reflection

What Is This Scripture Telling Me?

_____

_____

_____

_____

Why Did God Include This Scripture In The Bible?

_____

_____

_____

_____

What Do I Need To Further Study From This Verse?

_____

_____

_____

_____

Made in the USA
Coppell, TX
14 March 2020